Weather Update

Weather Forecasting

by Terri Sievert

Consultant:
Joseph M. Moran, PhD
Associate Director, Education Program
American Meteorological Society, Washington, D.C.

Capstone press

Mankato, Minnesota

Bridgestone Books are published by Capstone Press,
151 Good Counsel Drive, P.O. Box 669, Mankato, Minnesota 56002.
www.capstonepress.com

Library of Congress Cataloging-in-Publication Data
Sievert, Terri.
    Weather forecasting / by Terri Sievert.
    p. cm.—(Bridgestone books. Weather update)
    Includes bibliographical references and index.
    ISBN 0-7368-3739-6 (hardcover)
    1. Weather forecasting—Juvenile literature. I. Title. II. Series.
QC995.43.S54 2005
551.63—dc22   2004010857

Summary: Discusses the tools and methods used to forecast the weather.

Editorial Credits
Christopher Harbo, editor; Molly Nei, set designer; Linda Clavel, illustrator;
    Wanda Winch, photo researcher; Scott Thoms, photo editor

Photo Credits
Capstone Press/Karon Dubke, 4
Corbis/Jonathan Blair, 12
Courtesy of KEYC Television, 1
Dan Delaney Photography, cover (child), back cover
OneBlueShoe, 20
Photodisc/StockTrek, cover (background)
Tom Pantages, 6, 10, 14, 16, 18

1 2 3 4 5 6 10 09 08 07 06 05

Table of Contents

TOMORROW

Sunny Skies

Highs 85-90
Winds: NE 10-15

4

What Is Weather Forecasting?

What should you wear to school tomorrow? Will it rain on your picnic? A weather forecast can help you find out.

Weather forecasting is a way to **predict** the weather. People who forecast weather study weather maps and **radar** and **satellite** pictures. They look at temperature, wind speed, and wind direction. They use computers to turn this information into a weather forecast. This report tells people what kind of weather to expect in the days ahead.

◄ A TV weather forecaster predicts the weather for today and the days ahead.

Who Predicts the Weather?

Meteorologists are scientists who forecast the weather. They predict the weather for the coming days. They use tools to measure air temperature, wind, and rainfall.

All around the world, meteorologists are watching the weather. They let people know when storms are on the way. The National Weather Service forecasts the weather in the United States. The Meteorological Service of Canada forecasts the weather for Canada.

◄ Meteorologists with the National Weather Service use computers to study radar images of rain and snow.

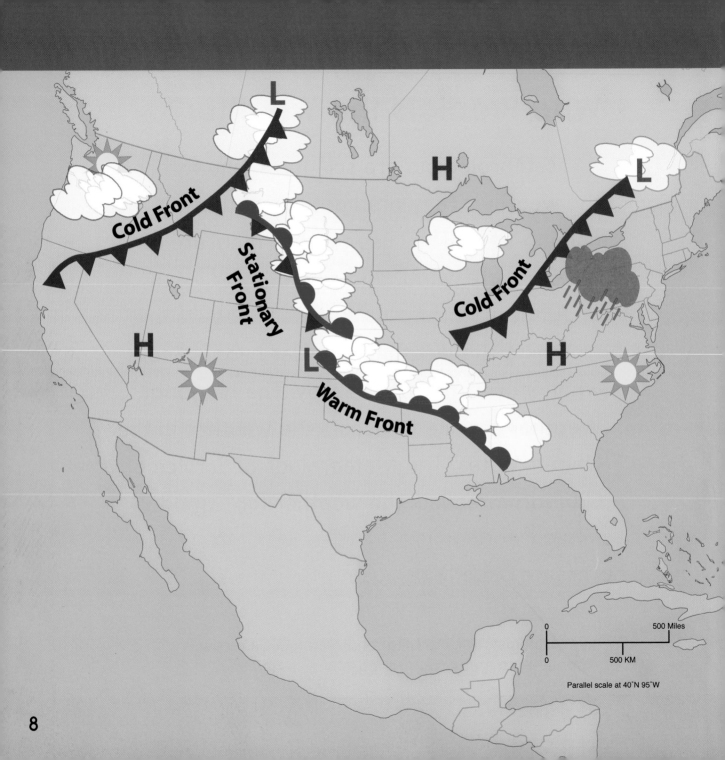

Weather Maps

Weather maps use symbols to show weather patterns in an area. Some symbols show fronts. A front is the leading edge of a warm or cold **air mass**. A line with half-circles is a warm front. A cold front is shown by a line with triangles. A line with triangles and half-circles is a **stationary** front.

Weather maps also show **air pressure**. An *L* means low air pressure. An *H* means high air pressure. Low air pressure often brings clouds and rain or snow. High air pressure usually brings fair weather.

◄ A weather map shows warm, cold, and stationary fronts. It also shows which areas are sunny, cloudy, or rainy.

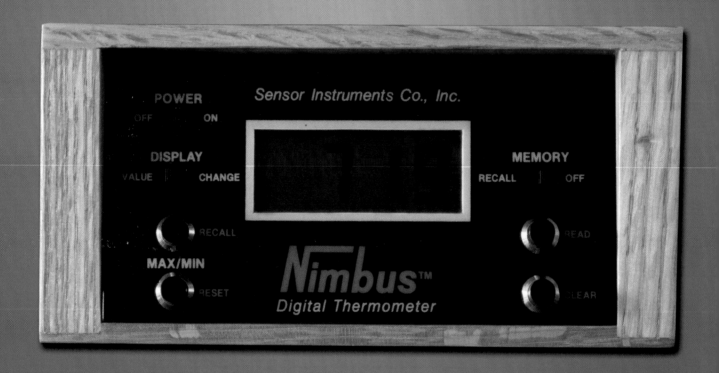

Thermometers

A thermometer is a tool that measures air temperature. Meteorologists use electronic thermometers and bulb thermometers.

An electronic thermometer measures air temperature with a sensor. The sensor is connected to a digital screen. The screen shows the temperature as numbers.

A bulb thermometer has a thin tube with a round end. Liquid in the tube expands and rises when the air warms. The liquid shrinks and falls when the air cools.

◄ An electronic thermometer shows the air temperature as numbers on a digital screen.

How Is Wind Measured?

Meteorologists measure wind direction and speed. Wind direction is found with weather vanes. Many weather vanes have an arrow connected to a rod. The arrow points in the direction wind is coming from.

Anemometers measure wind speed. An anemometer has three or four cups on a spoke. The spoke turns when wind hits the cups. A switch counts how often the spoke turns in a certain amount of time. An anemometer measures wind speed in miles or kilometers per hour.

◀ The cups on an anemometer spin to measure the wind speed during a snowstorm.

Barometers

A meteorologist measures air pressure with a barometer. This instrument shows when the weight of the air gets higher or lower. Some barometers show air pressure as a number on a digital screen.

Meteorologists watch for changes in air pressure. Changes in air pressure may mean the weather will change. Falling air pressure can mean rain or snow is on the way. Rising air pressure can mean fair weather is coming.

◄ A meteorologist checks the air pressure on an electronic barometer.

Rain Gauges

Meteorologists use rain **gauges** to measure rainfall. Tipping buckets are one type of rain gauge. When a tipping bucket collects .01 inch (.025 centimeter) of rain, its collection cup tips and empties. A switch counts how many times the cup tips.

A weighing gauge is also used to measure rainfall. It has a bucket attached to a scale. The scale records the weight of the rainfall. When the rain stops, the scale shows how much rain has fallen. The weight of the water is changed into inches or centimeters.

◀ The inside of a tipping bucket has a two-sided white cup that tips when rain fills it with water.

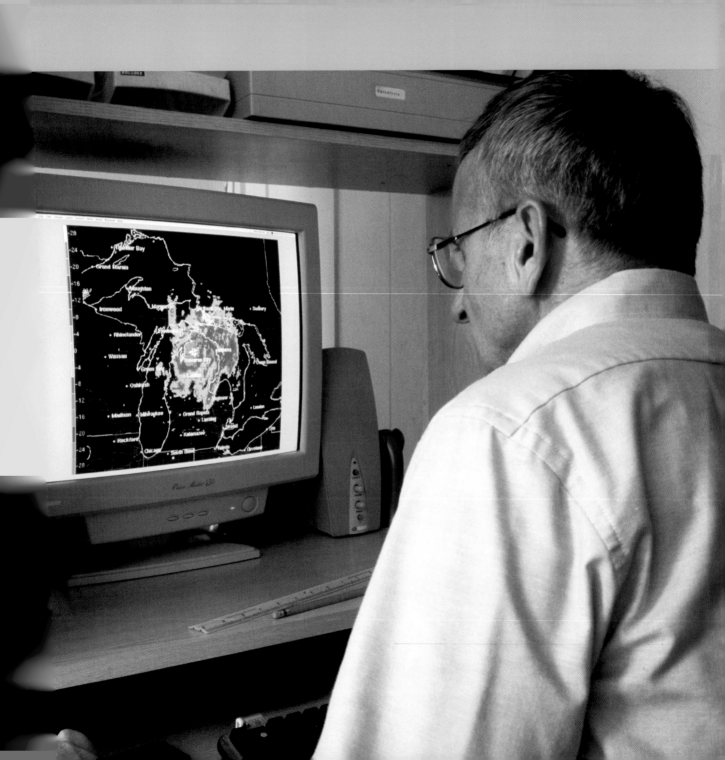

Radar and Satellite Pictures

Meteorologists use satellite pictures and radar to watch the sky. Satellites take pictures from far above the earth. These pictures show where clouds and storms are located.

Radar stations on the ground send out **microwaves**. The waves bounce off raindrops and snowflakes. Radar pictures can show how much rain or snow is in the clouds. It can also show how quickly a storm is moving.

◀ A meteorologist uses a computer to look at a radar image of rain falling over northern Michigan.

Forecast the Weather

Look at a weather map in a newspaper or on TV. What kind of weather is nearby? Where are the high and low pressure areas? Is a warm or cold front near your area?

Low pressure coming toward your area may bring rain or snow. Higher temperatures behind a front mean warmer weather is coming your way.

Reading the weather map can help you make your own forecast. What will the weather be like in the days ahead?

◄ Many newspapers print weather maps and daily forecasts to help people know what weather to expect.

Glossary

air mass (AIR MASS)—a huge volume of air that is uniform in temperature and humidity

air pressure (AIR PRESH-ur)—the weight of air on a surface

gauge (GAYJ)—an instrument for measuring something

microwave (MYE-kroh-wave)—an electromagnetic wave that is used in radar to locate precipitation

predict (pri-DIKT)—to say what you think will happen in the future

radar (RAY-dar)—a instrument that can find raindrops or snowflakes by sending out microwaves

satellite (SAT-uh-lite)—a device made by people that circles around earth; satellites often are used to gather weather information.

stationary (STAY-shuh-ner-ee)—not moving

Read More

Christian, Sandra J. *Meteorologists.* Community Helpers. Mankato, Minn.: Bridgestone Books, 2002.

Weber, Rebecca. *Weather Wise.* Spyglass Books. Minneapolis: Compass Point Books, 2003.

Internet Sites

FactHound offers a safe, fun way to find Internet sites related to this book. All of the sites on FactHound have been researched by our staff.

Here's how:
1. Visit *www.facthound.com*
2. Type in this special code **0736837396** for age-appropriate sites. Or enter a search word related to this book for a more general search.
3. Click on the **Fetch It** button.

FactHound will fetch the best sites for you!

Index